WOLF

BOB SCHURR

ISBN-13: 978-1482614985

ISBN-10: 1482614987

Dedication

I would like to dedicate this book, to my mother and father

Ralph and Mildred Schurr

I know it would have made them proud.

Acknowledgements

I would like to give thanks to the Menifee Valley Writers Group that I joined in 2012. I felt I had writing in me, but had trouble getting started until they shared their expertise and guided me. Special thanks to Mark Fletcher, of the group, who willingly and un-selfishly gives his expertise to us.

Cover designed by Mark Fletcher.

Forward

I first fell in love with wolves as a child, reading Jack London books, like Call of the Wild, and White Fang

I lived in the mountains of Big Bear Valley Ca. for thirty years. We had a wonderful dog, named Kimo, that was thought to be part wolf, and people would always ask if he was. He was loving and super smart. He would rub his head against me to show affection, like wolves do. We took many walks in the forest over his sixteen year life. We were very close, and I gained a lot of insight into his thoughts and feelings which helped with this story.

I had a long time dream inside me, of living in the forest and making contact with a wolf, which never happened. But the story was born.

Chapter 1
Lobo Negro

He awoke to a nearby sound. His ears, turning from side to side, were listening intently for something out of order. His sharp sense of smell told him that everything was all right. He stood up, stretched, yawned, and stepped out of his den. The smell of the dew, being warmed by the morning sun, gave him pleasure. There was an empty feeling in his stomach, so he loped off looking for something to eat.

In the distance he saw a deer. He knew it was up wind from him, because the wind was blowing from the deer to him, so he was sure he had not yet been detected. Crouching down slowly moving forward, using all the brush for cover, he moved ever closer. He waited till it was looking away, and was busy eating the grass. Then he shot forward, in a burst of speed that caught the deer, before she knew what hit her. After howling, and leisurely eating his catch, he sat down contentedly, licking his mouth until it was clean.

Lobo Negro was a young two year old timber wolf, just reaching maturity. His coat was a deep, shiny black, and his glowing yellow eyes, gave him a wild ominous look. Timber wolves are normally a pack animal, but after leaving his mother, he decided to be a loner. He still visited the pack and was accepted, but he didn't like having to bow down to the alpha male, the pack leader. Now that he was reaching maturity he was noticing an attraction to the females and only the pack leader was allowed to mate.

He had learned that the bears and the mountain lions were very powerful, and needed to be respected and avoided. And probably the worst, but not as common, were the ones that walked on their hind legs, and carried the barking stick that could kill from far away. These needed to be avoided at all cost, and he kept widening his range to find new territories. Today he came over a hill, looking into a new valley that showed no sign of them. He trotted down into the valley to explore.

On his way across the valley, Lobo Negro had chased down a prairie dog and ate it. After continuing on, he found a stream, where he drank till he quenched his thirst. Following the stream for a couple of hours he came to a small lake. Along the edge of the lake, he found foot prints, and the scent of many different animals. It should be good hunting he thought. Continuing to explore along a high wall of the valley, he found a cave in the rocks. There was no fresh scent of other animals, so he decided this would be home. It was a perfect den. Located high above the valley, he could see for miles. After a smaller opening the cave was just tall enough for him stand up in, about five feet deep and four feet wide. He had so far been exploring in day light, although wolves are mainly a nocturnal animal. So he lay down to sleep the rest of the day, and would hunt tonight.

The cool, moist smell of night awakened him. He stood up, stretched, stepped out of the cave and sat down to listen. Sensing everything was all right he stood up, urinated in front of the cave to mark his territory, and trotted off to find food. He frequently stopped along the trail to mark his new territory, as he went. He heard something moving in the brush to his right. He froze, looked, listened and felt a light breeze on his face. Knowing he was in a good position, he slowly crouched down and waited. A few minutes passed, and he heard whatever it was coming closer. Now the shape was forming, it could be a prairie dog or a porcupine. Knowing what would happen, if he grabbed a porcupine, he waited till he was sure. In the same instant he saw it was a prairie dog, he exploded into the air landing squarely on top of it. He threw back his head, and let out a long powerful howl. It seemed to last forever. He thought he heard a howl answering in the distance. After eating his kill, he headed back to his den. He had traveled several miles on his hunt, so it took a while to get there. The sun was coming up as he reached his den, so he lay down contentedly and fell asleep.

Lobo Negro opened his eyes. It was so bright he thought it was still daylight. He stood up, stretched, yawned, and stepped out of his den. There was a full moon, and no clouds. It almost looked like daylight. He looked up at the huge white moon, let out a series of howls, and sat down to stare in wonder. He again heard a faint howl from far away. This time he was sure of it, although it was too faint to tell where it came from. He started off in a different direction tonight, stopping occasionally, to mark his trail. This nightly hunting pattern went on successfully as the months rolled by. It had now been a year, since he settled in this valley. Male timber wolves can weigh up to one hundred seventy five pounds, and Lobo Negro was now reaching this, truly a formidable creature. He continued on his hunt, until he came upon a deer. The deer took off running, but he could run up to forty miles an hour, and quickly caught the deer. Howling to boast of his kill, he started to eat. When he heard a howl, this time, close by.

Chapter 2
She Wolf

Startled by the howl, he stopped eating to wait, watch and listen. Soon a grey, three year old female wolf, stepped out of the brush. She looked tired and hungry. Lobo Negro, backed away from his kill, and sat down. Letting her know, it was alright for her to eat. She had been with a wolf pack, where the alpha male tried to mate with her, and she wouldn't allow it. So she was forced out, and had been wandering on her own since then. After eating, she moved away from the kill, laid down and fell asleep. Lobo Negro sensed that she needed space, and stayed away from her. He finished eating, and lay down to keep watch over her, until she woke up.

When she woke up, she looked around and saw Lobo Negro. He was lying at a safe distance, so he would not be intimidating. When she got up and stretched, he stayed lying down, so she could make the first move. She slowly walked over and touched noses, so they could smell each other, and become more familiar. She seemed to be relaxed, so he got up and slowly walked away. He looked back over his shoulder, to see to see if she was following. She had sat down, and was not, so he gave a soft whine and started to walk again. The next thing he knew, she was walking along side of him at his shoulder.

Lobo Negro was thirsty, and knew she must be, so he headed for the stream. The stream was a mile or two away, so he broke into a trot. She stayed alongside of him as if they were one together. They reached the stream, and both drank their fill. Then she jumped into the stream and rolled around, as if trying to wash the dust of her travels off and start fresh. She got out of the stream and shook all the water off, and had a look on her face like she was smiling and content. The sun was up now, so they loped off to the den. When they arrived, he walked in and lay down, and she beside him. It was obvious they were a couple for life.

Now that there were two of them, their hunting style would change. They would of course need more food, and the two of them could bring down larger game. As night time fell, they set out on their first

hunt together. A short
distance from the den,
they came upon a
clearing where a few elk
were grazing. She Wolf
stayed where she was
and Lobo Negro moved

farther around the clearing. They both
stayed behind the cover of brush, downwind
from the elk, and each knew automatically,
to go after the smallest of the elk. Like being
released by a starter pistol, they shot into the
clearing. Lobo Negro, being bigger and
heavier, grabbed the elk by the back leg,
bringing it down. She Wolf went for the
throat to kill it. Then they began a howling
session that would give you chills and goose
bumps, telling the world what they had
done. After eating their fill, Lobo Negro
urinated around the elk to mark the
territory, and then they returned to the den.
Tomorrow they would go back to finish it.

The pair returned in the morning to finish their kill. There was a coyote eating the elk. He ran away as they approached, and would not be back, as coyotes don't like to stay in an area where there are wolves. They finished the elk, and sat down licking their mouths and each other's as a sign of affection. Afterwards they loped off to the stream to drink. Then started running around, playing like pups, enjoying the day and each other. They ran all the way back to the den, and flopped down, panting, content, and happy. After catching their breath, they fell asleep till nightfall.

It was now January, and mating usually occurs in the first few months, and pups are born in the spring. Lobo Negro and She Wolf were destined to start their own pack. When She Wolf knew pups were coming, she was realizing the den they were now in was not right for raising a family. There was no safe place for the pups to play in front of the den. No grass and foliage and trees to hide them from predators. She whined, got up and trotted off to look for such a place, with Lobo Negro right behind her. Not far down the slope from the den, there was a flat grassy area surrounded by forest. She looked around and found an old den from some other animal. There was no fresh scent, so she knew it was uninhabited. She got right to work digging the den larger to suit their needs. After about an hour or so, she stopped, and Lobo Negro got to work helping her while she rested. Several hours later they felt it was large enough for now, and after he marked the new territory, they both crawled in and fell asleep.

During the next few days, they put the final touches on the new den, in between hunting and sleeping. Lobo Negro missed his old den, and would sometimes go up and sit just watching over the valley. The gestation period for wolves is nine weeks. As it got closer to the end, She Wolf would stay by the den more and more, and let Lobo Negro do the hunting. This he did not mind at all. He would catch and eat something for himself, and then catch something and bring it home for her. Sometimes while she was resting, he would go out exploring around the valley. Having an instinct to travel his territory, and learn of any changes and new animals. In all his travels he would stop often, to mark his territory. This took a few days, off and on, while checking on She Wolf, and bringing her food.

It was now getting close to time for the pups to come, so he stayed close to the den. When hunting, he would catch the food, and bring it back to the den, for both of them to eat. The time for the pups to come, was now here, and She Wolf was in the back of the den, giving birth to five little future wolves. As they were born, she instinctively knew she must lick the fetal sack from their head so they can breathe. She also knew to lick the pups clean and eat the placenta, this giving her a meal while she is nursing. She Wolf kept the den and the pups clean licking up all their excretions, so it was odor free.

After a few days, she would come out, quickly relieve herself, eat a little that Lobo Negro had brought her, and hurry back to her babies, which were born deaf and blind, and completely dependent on her. This routine went on a few weeks, and now the pup's eyes were open and they were ready to come out of the den. Now, at last Lobo Negro will meet his five little bundles of mischievous pups. While the pups and their father were getting to know each other, She Wolf trotted off to the stream. She drank in peaceful bliss, for a long while. Then she rolled in the water washing off the many days of den, birthing and pups. Not wanting to be apart for too long, she trotted back to her family.

Chapter 3
Wolf Pack

The days, weeks and months that followed, were all a new experience for Lobo Negro and She Wolf. They would take turns hunting, while the other stayed behind with the pups. Lobo Negro loved staying with the little ones, watching them play, having them climb all over him, and chewing on his fur. He was a one hundred and seventy five pound mountain, and they were five little balls of multicolored fur. There was a black male, a black and grey male, a brown male, and two white females. This is the color pallet of what is now a seven member wolf pack. When She Wolf stayed with the pups, she of course would feed them, clean them, and sleep with them.

As the pups grew and were done with mother's milk, the parent would come home from the hunt, and regurgitate fresh meat for them to eat. It

would not be long, before the parent that was hunting would bring back a whole kill for the family to eat together. The pups love to play. They will play with each other, with the parents and with "toys" such as bones, feathers and animal skins. They will sneak up on them, pounce, bite and carry them around like trophies. These are skills they will use when they start hunting. The pups were now about eight weeks old, and would go with their parents to a rendezvous site, where they will stay while one or both of the adult wolves are hunting. Soon they will be six months old and will go on the hunt with the parents. The pups are already starting to catch lizards and small rodents like mice, to eat. As they learn more and more about being quiet, calm and stealthy when hunting, they are able to catch larger game birds. Next, as they get faster, they will start catching rabbits, and other small game.

The time had come for the pups to go along on their first hunt. When they got to the rendezvous site, this time She Wolf encouraged them to go along. In the past the pups would start to play when they got there, as they did now. Lobo Negro gave a quick low growl, and a look that could kill, the pups quickly got quiet and serious. For the first time, this wolf pack was going together on a hunt. The parents stopped, noses in the air, the pups did the same. They smelled elk up wind not too far away. Moving slowly off in that direction, they could see them about a quarter mile away.

The pups were anxious and nervous. She wolf gave them a quick low growl, and sharp look that settled them down. They approached the elk slowly, behind the cover of brush. When they got very close, the black male pup, Hunter, dashed towards a small elk. Lobo Negro and She Wolf quickly caught up with him and joined the attack, and the whole pack brought down the elk. They all began to howl, the pups were thrilled with the hunt, and the howling, they kept it up for quite a long time.

When the howling finally ended, they all began to feast on their kill. This was a new and exciting experience for the pups that were quickly becoming wolves. It had been a long and productive hunt, and the pack started back to the den to rest. As evening was approaching, Hunter woke up, stretched and started to howl, letting the pack know it was time to hunt. The rest of the pack woke up, stretched and started howling too. When they finished, Hunter trotted off ahead of the rest. Lobo Negro and She Wolf let him go on, to see how he would do. Hunter was very thirsty, so he went in the direction of the stream. When they reached it and drank their fill, he put his nose to the air, to search for the scent of game. Hunter knew he smelled something, but was not yet experienced enough to know what it was. He trotted off in that direction, to find out. As the scent got stronger he slowed down, creeping quietly towards it. Seeing ahead through the brush, there were a few deer grazing. He shot out towards the largest buck, with the brown male, not to be outdone, at his side. But he had started from too far away, and was not yet as fast as a mature wolf, so the buck got away. This kind of mistake went on for a while, as the young wolves learned how to hunt successfully.

The brown male, Timber, had now gotten into the spirit of the hunt. The third male Granite, was right with the pack, but did not try as hard as Timber. Neither did Blanca and Snow, the two white females. As the hunts went on, for they do every day, all of the other young wolves got into the hunt, and all had their times of victory. The pups are now getting close to a year old, and that is when they leave their mother, but not necessarily leave the pack.

Now that the pups were adults, Lobo Negro, was more and more drawn to his old den. He would go up and sit contentedly, just looking over the valley, and enjoying the solitude. This time when he went up and sat down, he found She wolf sitting next to him, as if to say, not without me. He turned his head toward her, and licked her muzzle, showing her, she was welcome. From then on, when he went up to the den, she was always with him. It didn't change the feeling of solitude, for they were as one. Sometimes, but not always, they would go out hunting by themselves, without the pups. Then sometimes it was reversed, and the five young wolves would go without them, showing their independence.

Chapter 4
Stands Alone

Now that the young wolves were mature
and independent, Lobo Negro was going
out looking to widen their hunting territory.
Sometimes She Wolf would go with him, as
she did this time. They went over the hills to
the east of them, and found another large
valley. Looking down they could see smoke
coming from inside the trees, on the far
side. There was a lot of area to cover, so
they were running at a fast, but not

exhausting pace. An hour or so later, as they were approaching the area where they saw the smoke, they slowed down to be more careful. The smoke was coming from a tall thing that was wide and round at the bottom, and came to a point at the top, with sticks coming out. The wolves sat and watched for a long time, wanting to know more of this thing.

After a while they heard something coming through the brush to their right. When it appeared, it was one of the ones that walked on their hind legs, and was carrying a dead deer over its shoulder. Lobo Negro noticed it was not carrying a barking stick, and he had heard no noise. It was carrying a long curved stick, and there was something on its back with short sticks in it. This one looked different than the ones he had seen in the past, his skin was a dark reddish brown, and not white like the others. Lobo Negro did not feel threatened by this one, and did not think he was dangerous. What he did not know, is that this was an Indian, who felt that the wolf was his brother. The Indian's name was Stands Alone, because from the time he was a boy, he was happy to be by himself. When he became a man, he left the tribe to live a life by himself, so that is why they gave him the name. The two wolves knew they did not have to worry about this one. He was living peacefully with the world, just hunting to feed himself.

Lobo Negro had not smelled the scent of any other wolves, on this journey, so on the way home he stopped occasionally to mark this new territory. They had traveled a good distance, and were in no hurry to get there. They found a safe place to lie down and sleep till dark. When the cool evening came, they stood up, stretched, and would hunt on the way home. After loping along, for two or three miles, they stopped. The smell of deer in the area had reached their noses. They carefully studied the situation, their senses telling them that the deer were up wind to their right.

The smell was strong, so the deer were not far away. The pair walked slowly towards them, until they could see a few through the brush. Creeping along as close as they could, without being seen, they leaped out of the brush at full speed. The deer was caught at the same second it saw them. After a short howling session, Lobo Negro and She Wolf had a good meal, and started off again on the trip home. After a short time they came upon a small stream, and leisurely drank their fill. They started off again at a good steady pace.

The sun was coming up and they were nearly home, so they kept up the fast pace, and would sleep when they arrived. Approaching the den, Lobo Negro noticed the scent of new wolves, mixed with their five. He felt it would be best to not disturb them, and check it out tonight. So they went up to the old den, and fell asleep.

That night, he and She Wolf awoke, to the howling of the pack, to start the hunt. They ran down to join the other wolves, and found that two new females had joined the pack, while they were away. This was fine with Lobo Negro and She Wolf, they seemed to fit in. Hunter, had taken over the role of alpha male, while they were gone, and Lobo Negro found he really didn't care, one way or the other. So with Hunter in the lead, the pack of nine wolves trotted off to find game. With nine hungry mouths to feed, they were looking for, *big game.*

A couple of miles away from the den, Hunter stopped. He had caught the smell of elk, as did Lobo Negro. Knowing that they were up wind, they started off slowly in that direction. The elk were still quite a ways away, but they needed to be quiet and stealthy. It seemed like forever, when they were finally in sight. There was a large male closest to them, and in one of the miracles of nature, they all knew which one, and sprang into action as one. It's hard to imagine, what nine charging wolves would look like to the elk, but they got the job done. As always they broke into a howling chorus, to celebrate the kill, and had a good meal. The pack stopped at the stream on the way back, to drink and continued back to the den. Since there were now more wolves, Lobo Negro and She Wolf, went up to the old den, which they preferred, anyway.

As the weeks went by, the hunting routine went on, the way it always does.

Lobo Negro and She Wolf seemed more and more to prefer to be alone, separate from the pack, since they were functioning fine without them. They decided to go back to the valley where they had seen the Indian. This was a pleasure trip, and they were in no hurry. They slept during the day, and traveled at night, hunting as they needed food. Lobo Negro had marked the trail, coming back on the last visit, so it was easy to follow. The first night out, they had traveled about ten miles, when they caught the scent of deer. They stopped, their keen senses telling them, where and how to proceed. They started off in that direction, slowly stalking their prey. When they came in sight, the deer closest to them, looked like a good size to feed them both. They shot out of the brush together, the deer bolted away, but they had no trouble running it down. As always, they howled for a short time, for a successful hunt. After feeding, they trotted contentedly off on their way. As the sun was coming up they found a space in a thicket, where they fell asleep until night fall.

When it was night, they awoke, stood up, stretched, yawned, licked each other's muzzle, and trotted off again. The pair picked up their speed as they went along. Sometimes it just feels good to run. The wolves at times, ran up to forty miles an hour. If they kept up the pace, they would reach their destination by morning. After a while, they stopped at a stream to drink. While she was drinking, She Wolf saw a large beaver, chewing on some branches across the stream. It was obvious the beaver had not noticed their presence, so she slowly crossed the stream. Sneaking up behind him within pouncing distance, she made a long leap, grabbing the beaver by the neck. This was not a full meal for the pair, but it would sustain them for now. Starting off again, they had eaten, quenched their thirst, and with the help of a full moon, were running to their destination.

Lobo Negro and She Wolf, had reached the top of the mountain, looking down into the valley, where they had seen the Indian. By sunrise, being in no hurry to continue, they found a vacant cave, where they would stay till night. A little tired from the run, and very contented with each other, they fell asleep. As the sun gave way to night time, the pair awoke, stood, stretched, and started down the hillside. It wasn't far, when the breeze brought them the smell of elk. The wind was blowing to them from the elk, so they knew they were down wind, where the elk could not smell them. Approaching ever so slowly, seeing a smaller cow, just right to feed them, they ran in after her. The startled elk, all took off in different directions. A large male, with his head down, charged straight at them, they split up, each running around him on different sides. Catching up with the female, Lobo Negro grabbed a hind leg, and She Wolf the neck. They had killed the cow, but the bull came charging back at them, so they had to run off and wait till he left. Then slip back quietly and eat their kill. This meal filled them up, and they were tired, from all the excitement, so they lay down to rest for a while.

After resting for about an hour, they got up and started off again on their journey, stopping now and then for Lobo Negro to mark his territory. He was going back to where they had seen the Indian, because he was curious and intrigued, about this one that did not seem to be dangerous. Stands Alone, appeared to be living life as they did, only killing to feed himself, and not bothering anyone else. Along the way they crossed a stream, where they drank, and traveled on. An hour or two later, they were near their destination, but were tired, so they found an area of dense brush and crawled in to sleep. Awakening while it was still daylight, they crawled out of the brush, and started off at an easy run. It wasn't long before they reached the clearing where Stands Alones' tepee was.

The pair stopped, while they still had the cover of brush, but could see through it to watch. The Indian was sitting outside, tanning the hide of a deer he had killed to eat. He would make clothes and moccasins from the skin, so nothing was wasted.

While the wolves were watching him, they were not aware, that he knew that they were there. He was happy that his brother wolves had come to visit. He started talking to them in a soft, warm voice.

"I am honored, that my brother wolves have come to visit me. You need not be afraid. I will not hurt you, and would like to see you more clearly."

The wolves, as if they knew what he was saying, stepped out of the brush. They also wanted to see him more clearly, for he seemed to be, like another friendly wolf. They sat down to watch and listen, to this one that was so different, but did not seem so.

"I have always wanted to visit with my animal friends like this. The Great Spirit must have looked favorably on me, to grant me this wonderful thing."

Lobo Negro felt comfortable with the meeting, and decided they would stay in this valley.

It was getting dark, and the wolves moved off to go hunting for food, but knew they would be back for another visit. Since Lobo Negro felt the Indian was like another wolf, he didn't want to hunt close to his area, and ran far off, away from him. Five or so miles away, they scented elk, but the breeze was blowing away from them towards the elk. So they had to circle around to where they would be down wind and the elk could not smell them. After making a big circle around where the elk were, they could feel the breeze on their face, and knew they were down wind. The scent of the elk was now strong, so moving slowly and quietly, the wolves crept forward. Upon seeing the elk through the brush, they leapt out of cover at full speed, and easily brought down the closest one. After eating their fill, and Lobo Negro urinating around the kill, they found a place close by where they could sleep and watch over their meal for tomorrow, because enough was left

Sleeping through most of the day, they awoke while it was still light, stood up, stretched, and rubbed against each other in a show of affection. Then trotted back to their kill, from the night before, where it was still intact. After leisurely eating the rest of the kill, they set out to explore, stopping occasionally for Lobo Negro to mark the area. Heading across the valley to the other side, they continued up the hill. From there, they saw a lake, off to their left in the bottom of the valley. In the other direction, was the Indian's tepee.

The pair started back down, in the direction of the lake. Picking up speed as they ran, and darting around things, like pups playing tag. Reaching the lake, they lie down panting till they caught their breath, so they could drink. Across the lake at the far end, there was a stream going up to the end of the valley. Trotting around the lake, they went up the other side, and then turned off to their right for a ways, till it was getting close to morning. They lie down under a tree behind some brush, and slept till night.

Chapter 5
More to Come

The place where they slept was a flat area in front of a hillside, where there was a hollowed out area that with a little work would make a good den. She Wolf woke up in the morning and started digging to make it larger for a den, for she now knew that pups were coming. Lobo Negro was not sure if she just wanted to make a new home, or if another litter was on the way. While she was digging, he trotted off to find if there was water, closer than the lake. He had not seen water, while they were coming to this place, so he went back in the direction they had come last night

A short way past where they came up the hill, he found a small pond, fed by a spring. They had found a perfect place to make a new home. When he got back to the den, She Wolf had finished digging, and was lying outside panting from the work. He gave a short bark, to let her know to follow, and trotted off to the pond. She was very happy to find water, and after drinking her fill, rolled around in the water, to wash off the dirt. She came out and shook off the water, and ran off to the den to sleep the rest of the day, with Lobo Negro beside her.

As the heat of the day, turned to the cool of night, they woke up in their new den. Moving outside, they sniffed the air, to make sure everything was as it should be, and then howled for a short time to start the hunt. Heading down towards the lake, where they had seen animal tracks the night before, the scent of deer on the ground stopped them. The scent on the ground, masked any in the air, so they followed it. Moving very slowly, and checking now and then for a breeze, it seemed to be dead calm. They followed the trail, listening intently for any sound, until they heard something moving in the brush. Standing dead still, with eyes straining to see any movement, they saw shadows moving. When there is no breeze at all, it's hard to tell who has the upper hand. So they crawled, very slowly, towards the moving shadows. Finally, the shadows became deer, and without hesitation, they sprang into action. As the deer started to run away, they caught the closest one, and brought it down. Howling for their success, and then having a good meal, they trotted off to the pond near their den. Quenching their thirst, they took their time going back to the den.

As time went by, and She Wolf was getting closer to having pups, she would go along on the hunt, but did not participate. Lobo Negro would make the kill, and they both would eat. Soon, it was getting very close, and she would stay at the den, and he would bring food back for her. Tonight, Lobo Negro caught a deer. After he ate, he carried the rest back to the den for her. This time, she was not waiting outside for him, as usual. He dropped the rest of the deer, caught his breath, and heard the sound of pups in the den.

Knowing she would not leave the pups right away, he slept outside to guard the kill. In the morning, she came out and ate, trotted down to the pond to drink, and hurried back to the den. Before she went in she stopped and licked Lobo Negro on his muzzle. This litter, she had only two pups, and he could tell by the sound, there weren't many. This routine of him hunting, and bringing back food for her, went on for the next few weeks. The pups had opened their eyes after two weeks, and were just starting to walk, after three weeks.

This night when he came back to the den, she was waiting outside, with the pups, and he could see there were only two. Before she ate, she went to the pond to drink, and rolled in the water, to wash off the time spent in the den. Shaking off the water, she ran back to the den, where Lobo Negro, was licking the pups as they stumbled around his legs. There was a black and grey male, and a grey female. This was an easy birth, with not a lot of trouble, taking care of them. After she ate, she regurgitated some of the meat for the pups, who were now starting to eat solid food. As with the last litter, Lobo Negro was enjoying the pups climbing on him, and chewing on his fur. It wasn't long, before the pups were running around, fighting with each other, and playing with pieces of bone, or whatever they could find. Soon they were going out with the parents, and chasing anything that moved, like lizards, bugs and mice.

Now the time had come, to go to a rendezvous place, where the pups would wait, with one of the parents, while the other hunted. She Wolf wanted to hunt, as she had not been getting much exercise for a while, so Lobo Negro stayed with the pups. The pups were busy, chasing anything that moved, which was good training for learning to hunt. When they couldn't find anything, they chased each other, stalking one another, like they were hunting, then pouncing on their prey. While they were busy, She Wolf was busy hunting. She had tracked a couple of deer, and was sneaking within striking distance. She was as close as she dared, without being seen. Her body bunched up, like compressing a spring that shot her out of the brush to the closest deer. She grabbed the back leg as it ran, then stopped, throwing it to the ground, then jumped on its' neck for the kill. She howled, to let Lobo Negro know, of her success. He came running, with the pups bounding along behind, excited to be part of this. They all had a good meal, and stopped at the pond to drink, on the way to the den. The pups of course, jumped in the water to play, and had to be dragged out, to continue back.

The next morning, Lobo Negro decided it was time to go and visit the Indian, since the pups were now big enough to travel the distance. He started off with the pups behind him, and She Wolf was at the rear, to keep the pups in line. It was six or seven miles to his tepee, but they were in no hurry and Lobo Negro just went at a trot, so the pups could keep up. The pups were having no trouble, and they came up to be on each side of him. Then She Wolf came up to join them, and they trotted along four abreast. The wolf pack stayed this way, splitting apart, for an occasional rock or bush, until they arrived. They didn't bother to stay in the cover of the brush, since they were now comfortable with the Indian. They just appeared, and sat down, the pups not knowing what to make of this strange site. Stands Alone, was sitting in front of his tepee, smoking his pipe. He was just amazed, at what he saw.

"I cannot believe what I am seeing. My brother wolves have honored me again, coming back with a family. I am truly blessed."

The pups were amazed, at this strange creature talking to them. But since they were still learning of the world around them, they accepted it as just another thing to learn.

"Your children are beautiful. I would like to know them better."

The black and grey male, being the bolder of the two, walked up to inspect this creature closer. The Indian held out his hand, the pup smelled it and sat down, trying to absorb all of this.

"You honor me with your presence, little one. I will call you, *Spirit,* as the Great Spirit must have sent you to me, to be my friend. And what of you *Little Sister,* I guess you are content to stay with your parents?"

The Indian, once again, held out his hand to *Spirit,* who licked it, and went back to his family.

The wolves now turned, and disappeared into the brush, just as they had come.

About halfway back to the den, as night was falling, they saw some rabbits, up ahead, that had come out to eat the grass. The wolves were downwind, from the rabbits, and they had not yet been smelled, or seen. The parents quickly crouched down, and the pups watching them, did the same. Lobo Negro and She Wolf started slowly crawling forward, with Spirit and Little Sister doing the same. When they were close enough, the parents darted out and each caught a rabbit, with the stunned pups staying behind. This being their first hunt, they had now seen what to do. The adults let the pups eat the rabbits, so they could see the reward of the hunt, and of course there was not enough for all of them.

Starting off again, on the way back, Lobo Negro and She Wolf, still needed food, so they kept a slow pace, senses tuned for any sound or scent. Getting close to the den, they got the scent of elk. The breeze was bringing it to them, so they knew they were not yet detected. The pups, now knowing what the hunt was all about, sensed it too. Cautiously, the pack moved in the direction of the scent. It was not long, before they could see the elk, through the brush. Inching along on their bellies, as far as they could without being seen, they sprang out at full speed. Running down the closest elk, with the pups close behind, they made the kill. The pups got there in time, to feel they were helping, and had performed perfectly, stalking the prey. They all joined in, for a well- deserved howling session, which the pups kept up for quite a long time. The den was not far, so they dragged the remainder of the elk, back to the den, after eating their fill. It had been a long day and night, and the wolves were very tired. They lie down together in the den and quickly fell asleep.

Sleeping through the day, they awoke the next evening, and crawled out of the den. The pups were wound up, with the energy of the young, running around and chasing each other. Lobo Negro and She wolf were hungry, and had started eating the elk, from last night. When Spirit and Little Sister saw them, they quickly joined in, fearing there might not be any left for them. After eating and licking their mouths contentedly, the wolves rubbed against each other, in a show of affection, then trotted off to the pond to drink. Since they didn't have to hunt tonight, the pack did some exploring, down to the lake. Lobo Negro, stopped now and then, to urinate, and mark his area, and of course, Spirit, did the same as his father.

After reaching the lake, they walked along the shore for a ways, studying the ground, for the scent of other animals. This was like reading the newspaper for them, and learning of their surroundings. They soon came upon a bear, fishing along the lake. Spirit started to walk forward to investigate, and Lobo Negro gave a sharp bark, and snapped at him, letting him know, that this was an animal to be respected, and stay away from. The pack had come a long way, and it would take the rest of the night, to get back to the den, so they turned around and started home. They stopped at the pond to drink, along the way, and then went to their den to sleep.

The next evening, Lobo Negro and She Wolf woke up, to find the pups were already out of the den. Crawling out, they saw Spirit, and Little Sister, crouched down watching some rabbits. The rabbits had not seen them, motionless, and waiting. They saw their moment, and shot into the rabbits, each grabbing one. The pups, that were quickly becoming wolves, walked back to their parents, each with a rabbit in their mouth, and dropped them in front of Lobo Negro, and She Wolf. Then sat down and howled to their hearts content. Spirit, and Little Sister, each ate their rabbit, which were now only an appetizer, to the growing wolves.

The pack of four, started out into the night, hunting for bigger game. They had gone quite a ways, before they caught the scent of elk, nearby. Noses in the air, they assessed the situation, knowing their position, they slowly moved forward towards the scent. When the elk were in sight, there was a large female, closest to them. Inching within striking distance, the pack shot out of cover. The startled elk were quickly in flight, but not fast enough, to out run the wolves. The pack was all around the elk, each grabbing legs, neck, and throat, to bring it down. When the kill was done, they all howled, for a short while, and had a good meal. The contented wolves, started back to the den, stopping for water, on the way.

The weeks and months rolled by, with the routine of life and hunting, the wolf pack was working like a well-oiled machine. The pups were now a little over a year old. At that age the bond of motherhood is broken, but they are not fully mature until two years old. By then, Lobo Negro and She Wolf would be about eight years old. Timber wolves live to be less than ten years old, in the wild. So they will be getting closer to the other end of life, by then. Spirit, had never forgotten the Indian, and was now thinking of going back, for another visit, and so was Lobo Negro. It was strange, how father and son, had the same feeling, and they had both decided, it was time. The hunt last night had been a good one, and all the wolves were well fed. They had slept the rest of the night, and would leave in the morning.

Chapter 6
The Return

The morning was beautiful, it was cool, the skies above were clear, and it was a perfect day. Lobo Negro and Spirit, started off to go to their visit with the Indian, and She Wolf and Little sister followed, and somehow knew where they were going. They covered the miles to the Indian's tepee, at an easy, effortless run. When they arrived, Stands Alone, was nowhere in sight, so the wolves all laid down, to rest, and wait. It was not too long, before the Indian returned. He had been out hunting, and walked in out of the brush, carrying a deer, he had killed, on his shoulders.

Seeing the wolves, he dropped the deer, and said, "My brother wolves have again returned, and look how big the young ones have grown."

Spirit, immediately, got up and walked over to the Indian, and licked his hand.

"I am glad to see you too, Spirit my brother. Putting out his hand, he laid it on Spirits head. I see now, that we are truly friends."

Spirit sniffed at the deer, thinking that would be good to eat.

"My friends are probably all hungry, if you will stay, I will skin the deer, take the part I want, and give the rest to you."

Stands Alone, hung the deer up with a rope over a tree branch, then quickly, and expertly, skinned it and cut out the portion he wanted. Then he carried the rest, closer to the wolves, and dropped it on the ground. The wolves were not sure about this, but could not resist, something that smelled so good. So they all shared what was left, and licking their mouths, tried to absorb all of this, strange situation.

"Now we are all truly a family," the Indian said.

Lobo Negro, and the females, turned to leave into the brush, and realized that Spirit, was not coming. They knew he was of age, so they accepted it, and started on the journey back to the den.

"I see you are going to stay with me for a while, this makes me very happy."

Spirit, did not understand the words, but liked the sound of his voice. He lay on the ground, watching the Indian, as he went about smoking the meat. Stands Alone, cut off a portion to eat now, with a little extra for Spirit. As he ate, he would throw pieces to Spirit, which the wolf caught in the air.

Spirit was enjoying this time with the Indian, but was also missing the pack. So he stood up, licked the hand of his friend, and ran off after them.

"Goodbye, my brother, I know we are destined to meet again."

He watched the wolf disappear, knowing how lucky he was, to have experienced this wonderful thing.

Spirit, was running at full speed, up to forty miles an hour, he arrived back at the den, as the others were going out to hunt. He squeezed around, in and out them, licking their muzzles, as he did. They were as glad to see him as he was them. They went out to hunt, with Spirit panting to catch his breath, from the run. They all knew that at some future time, he would go back.

Heading out on the hunt, the pack went by the pond, because Spirit was very thirsty from his long run. After the wolves drank their fill, they kept going past the pond, because they hadn't hunted much, in this area, before. After a mile, or so, they caught the scent of deer in the area. Standing still, until they figured out where the wind was coming from, and which direction the deer would be in. The pack started out slowly towards where they should be. Finally seeing them in the distance, the four of them crept closer and closer. Just as they were in striking distance, one of the wolves stepped on a twig that snapped. Hearing this, the deer bolted off, they were startled, but didn't know what it was, and they hadn't seen the wolves. The pack was still motionless, the deer were startled, but didn't sense danger, so they stopped and started feeding again.

Everything was still in the pack's favor, and they again started stalking their prey. When they were in striking distance, and since the deer were small, the wolves ran out in pairs, each pair grabbing their closest animal. The pack, as always, howled for their conquest, and then fed on their prey. It is a wonder, how these perfect hunting machines, somehow communicate mentally, and know just what to do, in any situation. The males, as always, had been marking their trail, and followed it back to the pond, to drink. Then travelled on, back to the den, where four contented wolves, settled down to sleep.

Awakening the next evening, as they stretched, and moved outside, there was a strong scent of elk, which meant they must be close by. Taking their time reading the situation, the pack moved slowly in the direction where the elk must be. The wolves had not gone far at all, when they could see the elk through the cover of brush. Inching ever closer, the four jumped out of cover, running down a large female, that was closest to them. Spirit had out run his father, grabbing a back leg. Lobo Negro caught the other leg, and the females went for the neck, for the kill. The pack howled for such an easy hunt that was close to the den, and would feed them for a couple days. After eating their fill, Lobo Negro and Spirit, urinated all around their kill. This would keep most animals away till they came back tomorrow. The pack then went back to the den to sleep.

Chapter 7
A New Member

The next evening, the pack returned to the elk, they killed the night before. To their surprise, there was a female wolf lying just outside the marked area around the kill. She had apparently, so far, respected this, and had not gone in to eat. Lobo Negro walked over to her, and sniffed her nose, as she did him. The rest of the pack did the same after him, and there didn't seem to be any problem. The pack went over to the kill, ate their fill, then moved away and sat down. This was letting the new wolf know it was alright for her to eat. When she finished, she walked over to Spirit, and sniffed his nose, then licked his muzzle. This, letting Spirit know, she was interested in him. Since he was now fully mature, a little over two years old, and it was the beginning of mating season, apparently the pack had a new member.

Even though it was mating season, Lobo Negro and She Wolf, being the age they were, did not have any interest in having another litter. And Little Sister, just becoming mature, as was her brother, was in no hurry to find a mate. The new member, Cocoa, seemed to be about two to three years old. She was grey, with areas of brown on her head and back. She seemed to fit in with the rest of the pack, and there were no problems with any of the members. When they were all done eating, and getting to know each other, the pack of now five, headed off to the pond to drink. After quenching their thirst, they returned to the den, which was already full, and now would be a little fuller. Tomorrow, they would have to do a little digging to make it bigger. The pack woke up the next afternoon, to make the den a little larger. They all took turns digging, and in no time at all, it was done.

It was becoming early evening, as the pack started out to the pond, to drink and wash off the dirt from digging, then headed out into the night, to hunt. After a couple miles, the wind brought the scent of elk, to the wolves. Knowing they were in a good position to continue, they slowly and quietly proceeded, towards where the elk should be. There were a lot of small trees, and underbrush to hide them from sight, as the pack moved forward. When they could see,

there were seven or eight elk, and half were
large males, which could be very dangerous.
There was a fair distance, between cover
and the males that were on the downwind
side, so they couldn't go around, to the
females. It was a gamble, whether or not
they could get through the males, before
they defended them-selves. The pack ran
out as fast as they could, but the elk saw
them and had their heads down, with a lot
of dangerous antlers ready to strike the
wolves.

The pack had to turn
tail and run, and She
Wolf narrowly missed
the antlers, which
brushed her side, but
didn't cut. The four male
elk chased them back
into the brush, where they hid motionless,
to wait and see if there was another

opportunity. After about half an hour, the elk moved off, to regroup and start feeding again. The wolves followed them, at a safe distance for a while, but the wary elk, did not give them another opportunity. So they moved off to look for other game.

After about an hour of hunting, they saw deer in the distance. Moving around to stay downwind from the deer, the wolves started stalking their prey. When they had worked their way up to striking distance, they could see two bucks nearest to them. Darting out of cover, the pack gave chase, Lobo Negro and She Wolf went for the closest deer, he grabbed a back leg, and she the throat for the kill. Spirit, Little Sister, and Cocoa, ran down the other buck, for the kill. After some howling, the five wolves had a good meal, and started back to the den. It had been a long night of hunting, and the now very tired wolves, were quickly asleep.

This routine of life, the never ending cycle of hunting and living, went on for another month or so. Cocoa, the new member, was now pregnant with Spirit's pups. Soon, she would be digging a new den close by the packs den, where she would have her pups, but for now, she was still hunting with the pack. The wolves were awakening, and stretching, for another night of hunting, and she started the howling, for the hunt. Elk had been plentiful, in the area lately, and were a good size for five wolves. They were however, a couple of miles away, because of the odor of wolves around the den. After traveling a couple of miles from the den, the scent of elk was in the wind, coming from their right. So the pack turned in that direction, and slowly proceeded. Soon, they could see the heads of elk, going up and down above the brush, as they ate and watched. This was still about a quarter of a mile away.

Crouching down so they couldn't see the elk, which meant the elk, could not see them either, the pack slowly moved in that direction. They kept this up until the elk, were just visible, through the brush. Now they spread out five wide, and crawled inch by inch, till they could see well enough to plan their next move. Closest to them, was a large female, big enough to feed the pack. Shooting out of cover, the wolves grabbing legs or neck, quickly brought it down, and killed it. Then they all looked up, ready for charging males, as had happened before, and again did this time. The pack ran back into the brush, until they heard the elk stop, and then, so did they. After the elk moved off, they went back. Looking out of the brush and trees, the elk were not in sight, so they went back to their kill. After first howling for their success, the wolves had a well- earned meal.

Sitting and licking their mouths in content, the pack then loped off to the pond to drink, and back to the den. Spirit had noticed, that this was the fourth time he had beaten his father to the kill, when they attacked. Was Lobo Negro getting slower, from age, or just letting Spirit get there first?

Chapter 8
Another Den

This afternoon the wolves awoke to the sound of rain, and although it was still day, it was very dark. These conditions made it very hard to hunt, for they had to hunt by eyesight only. The senses of scent and hearing, did not work at all, in the rain. The pack stepped out into the rain, stretched, yawned, and started on the hunt. As they went, five pairs of eyes were looking everywhere for game. Even eyesight is greatly diminished in the rain, so when they did see game, they would already be close. About an hour later, moving slowly, Spirit saw an elk. He quickly crouched down, and the rest of the pack did the same. Moving very slowly, under the cover of trees and brush, the pack could see several elk ahead.

The only elk they could see clearly was a large female, closest to them.

Spirit, Little Sister, and Cocoa, Dashed out of cover, the females grabbed the hind legs and Spirit went for the neck. Lobo Negro and She Wolf were close behind to help finish the job. The pack quickly looked everywhere for charging males, but saw none. They stood motionless for a couple minutes, to make sure, and didn't howl for fear of drawing attention to themselves. The wolves were happy to make the kill in these conditions, and eating in the rain they also quenched their thirst. It's a good thing wolves have a strong sense of direction, because eyes and scent, were not much help, finding their way back to the den in the rain. They arrived at the den, trying to shake off as much of the rain as they could, before entering.

Cocoa was up early the next day, she was digging a new den, where she would have her pups. When the other wolves woke up, they came out, stretched, yawned, and started in helping with the digging. Spirit was first, because he now knew, Cocoa was going to have his pups. With all the wolves taking turns, it wasn't long before the den was done. The den went straight in, and then turned to the left, so Cocoa would be out of sight, when she had her pups. When the pack was done, and she was happy with the den, they went to the pond, to drink, and wash off the dirt. Night was now falling, and it was time to hunt. They started howling, then, left in search of game.

This night, they went down into the valley towards the lake, where they hadn't been for a while. The pack was most of the way down, when the scent of elk was in the breeze. The wind seemed to be coming straight at them, so maybe the elk, would be at the lake. When the wolves could see the elk, through the cover of brush, they were at the edge of the lake, drinking. There was too much open space, between their cover, and the elks. So the pack waited, until the elk moved off to find food. They quietly followed, being careful to stay downwind. The elk soon stopped to graze. Spirit had been watching a big female that was lagging behind the rest. The second she put her head down to eat, he, along with the rest of the pack, charged out to grab her, and bring her down.

Just as they finished, there was something crashing through the brush to their right. A male elk, unnoticed by the wolves, had drifted off from the rest, and was now charging right at them. The pack all split in different directions, trying to get out of the way. Lobo Negro was closest to its path, and

leapt out of its way, just missing sure death.
Spirit ran right through the group of startled
elk, and somehow didn't get trampled. The
wolves were just as startled as the elk. They
all ran a safe distance, then regrouped, and
stopped to catch their breath, and gather
their wits. After waiting awhile, and not
hearing any more sounds of the elk, they
slowly and carefully headed back to the kill.
When the pack returned to their kill, all was
quiet. There was no sign of the elk herd. So
they let out a few howls, and ate their meal.
After finishing, the pack headed back up the
side of the valley, to the pond near their
den. They drank their fill and returned to
the den. It had been a busy, exciting night
the wolves were tired, and went quickly to
sleep.

After the passing of a few more weeks, it
was getting close to the time for Cocoa to
have her pups. She went out with the pack

to hunt this night, but would not participate in the attack. The pack had been out for about an hour, when Little Sister, noticed a slight scent of deer in the wind, on the left side of her face. Turning in that direction, she continued at a trot, sensing that they were not yet that close. As the scent got stronger, the pack slowed down, moving closer, until they could see the deer feeding on the grass.

Spirit and Little Sister, being younger and faster, would go after a big buck, that was a little farther away. Lobo Negro and She Wolf would go after a doe, right in front of them. As the four sprang into action, leaving the pregnant Cocoa behind, Lobo Negro and She Wolf easily caught the doe, before it could run. The buck had taken flight, but the young pair quickly ran it down. The pack howled for a successful hunt, with Cocoa joining them, and ate their kill. The wolves were grateful for a smooth and easy hunt, and Lobo Negro and She wolf, were happy to bring down the deer, as old age was taking its toll on them.

The well-fed and contented pack, started back to the den, traveling at an easy pace, and stopping at the pond to drink. Another week went by, with Cocoa going on the hunt, but not participating in the kill. Then this night, she stayed at the den, and Spirit would bring her food. When the pack returned from the hunt, Spirit dropped a large chunk of meat on the ground, for Cocoa. After leisurely eating the food, Cocoa licked her mouth clean, then, after licking Spirit on the face, in appreciation, she went into the back of her den. Spirit stayed in the front of the den, and the rest of the pack retired to theirs.

Chapter 9
Pups Are Coming

The next day, late afternoon, Spirit awoke to the sound of pups. He moved out of the den, to leave Cocoa alone, with the birthing. In one of the marvels of nature, and even though this was her first litter, Cocoa knew she must lick the fetal sack from the pups head, letting it take its first breath. She also instinctively knew she must swallow these membranes, along with the placenta and umbilical cord. This also gave her a valuable meal, while she was nursing. She licked them dry and encouraged them to nurse. While nursing, she kept them clean and dry, by swallowing all their excretions. This also was keeping the birthing area clean, and odor free. When all was done, she had four new little wolves, three females and one male.

While Cocoa is taking care of her pups, the hunting is going to be mostly up to Spirit and Little Sister, and whatever help, the aging Lobo Negro and She Wolf can give. After some brief howling, the four headed out for tonight's hunt, with Spirit in the lead. Tonight, the pack started out to the left from their den, as it had been quite a while since they had explored this area. After about half an hour, the pack could sense there were deer in the vicinity, but the air was completely still, and they couldn't tell where. They spread out a little, and crept very slowly ahead, with all senses straining

for a hint of where the deer were. Spirit,
who was on the right side of the pack,
stopped dead still, he had caught a glimpse
of the deer to his right. The rest of the pack,
reading his body language as he stopped,
carefully moved in that direction. There
were five or six deer that had obviously not
sensed the wolves, as yet. There was a large
buck in front of Lobo Negro, facing away
from him, he would go for that. The pack
shot out into the deer. Lobo Negro grabbed
the back of the deer, like a one hundred
and seventy pound anchor, allowing for She
Wolf, to grab the neck, for the kill. Spirit
and little Sister, had run down another
buck, and were about seventy five feet away.
After happily howling for another success,
the pairs ate their respective kills, Spirit
leaving a big chunk for Cocoa. The males
urinated to mark the area, and the pack
headed back to the den, with Spirit carrying
the meat for Cocoa.

When the wolves returned to the den, Cocoa came out and quickly ate the meat. She then ran to the pond to drink, and after relieving herself, quickly ran back to her pups. This routine of hunting, and bringing back food to Cocoa, went on for another three weeks. The pups now had their eyes open and they were starting to explore the den. After a long night of hunting, the pack returned to the den, as the morning light was coming. Cocoa came out to meet them, and eat the food they had brought. While she was eating, the little wolves staggered to the front of the den, whining for their mother. Spirit lay down in the front of the den, and for the first time got to see his pups. They were a little wobbly, and climbing over his legs was still a bit of a struggle. They all looked more or less the same, except the male was a little bigger, and all were grey and black.

After eating, Cocoa took this time to leisurely trot to the pond to drink, and took her time coming back, while Spirit was watching the pups. This was a nice break from all the time in the den. When Cocoa returned, she took the pups back into the den, to nurse and sleep. Spirit lay down in the front of their den, the rest of the pack went into theirs, and all went to sleep, till the next night. When night came, Cocoa decided she would go on the hunt, and Lobo Negro would stay and babysit the pups. This is not unusual as wolf packs are very family oriented, and will take turns, watching the pups. This also was a good idea, because Cocoa is a younger and stronger hunter. The pack was ready, they howled briefly, and set out into the night. The pack headed back towards the same area as the last night, as the hunting was good, and they hadn't spent a lot of time in that part of the forest.

A few miles out, Cocoa, picked up the scent of elk, she paused briefly, making sure of the direction of the wind, and started out again in that direction. As the scent got stronger, and they knew they were getting close, the pack slowed down. Slowly inching ahead, with Cocoa in the lead, until she could see several elk, and they planned their next move. Closest to them, was a small male, the four wolves would all go for it. Leaping out of cover to the elk, Cocoa and Little Sister grabbed the hind legs, She Wolf a front leg, and Spirit the throat, for the kill. It took all their strength to hold on, till the elk fell. After a moment to catch their breath, and make sure they weren't being attacked. The wolves proudly howled, and consumed their meal. Spirit picked up a large portion for Lobo Negro, and they headed back to the den.

After a mile or so, Spirit stopped and dropped the meat, and Little Sister picked it up, to carry it the rest of the way. When they arrived at the den, Lobo Negro was in the front of the den, with the pups all curled up in between his legs against his chest. Lobo Negro got up, to come out and eat, and Cocoa took the pups back in the den to nurse. It was a good night for the wolves, and they all went off into a peaceful sleep.

They finished the next week, with either Lobo Negro or She Wolf, babysitting the pups, and the rest of the pack hunting. Now the little wolves were ready to eat meat, and make short trips outside the den. When the pack came back from the hunt, this night, She Wolf was outside with the pups. Cocoa lay down next to her pups, and they licked at her mouth, causing her system to regurgitate the meat she had eaten, into her mouth. The pups hungrily, ate the meat, from their mother's mouth, and went into the den to sleep.

Today Cocoa woke up midday, because she wanted the pups to enjoy the light and the sunshine. The pups loved being out in the daylight playing, they chased each other around, jumping and pouncing on one another. Actually learning some of the things they will use as adults. They would sneak up on pieces of bone, or whatever they could find, and then run and attack like hunters. It wasn't long before Spirit came out to play with his pups also. He enjoyed it every bit as much as the pups did. Especially the male, who was grabbing things and shaking them as hard as he could, and letting them fly wherever, then slowly sneaking up on them again, and jump on them once more. After a while the pups were tired, And Cocoa took them into the den to nurse and sleep.

Chapter 10
A great Loss

Cocoa kept up this midday to afternoon playing time for the next week or so, with the pups getting bigger every day. It had been six weeks, since the pups were born. Now they were able to take walks up to a mile away from the den, as they were doing today. The new little wolves of course, loved this, with all the new sights and sounds, around them. They picked up, and played with, every new thing they found along the way. It was truly a great adventure for them, and they couldn't wait for the next day to come. Cocoa took them a different way each day, so they could see more of the surrounding area, and explore more things every day. Spirit also took them, and he would stop and urinate along the way, to show the male how to mark his territory. The pup, Hunter, instinctively picked this up right away.

The next day, while Cocoa was watching them in front of the den, one of the females went running after a lizard too far away for safety. Cocoa immediately jumped up and ran after her, to bring her back. Just as she  was catching up to her, a large eagle swooped down out of the sky, catching the helpless pup in its long talons. The talons pierced her heart and lungs, killing her instantly. Cocoa, in the same second, had lunged at the eagle, grabbing it by the neck, and shaking it violently, in a rage of anger. The pup was released, too late, and the eagles head was torn from its body. Cocoa nuzzled the lifeless pup, knowing full well that it was dead. She started digging a hole in the ground where she stood, to bury her pup, so she didn't have to see it. Cocoa, and the rest of the pack, being a family, would mourn deeply for this tragic loss. She took her three remaining babies into the den, to nurse and be close to them. Spirit also went into the den, to be close to Cocoa and the three pups. He would also mourn, nearly as deeply as her, they eventually went to sleep. None of the pack would hunt that night.

They all awoke the next day, when they came out of the den, the eagle was nowhere in sight. Before going in the den last night Lobo Negro had taken the dead eagle away and buried it, so it would not have to be a grim reminder of that awful event.

As always life must go on, though the grief would be there, the wolves would have to function and hunt. The pack had missed a day of food, so they started out when it was still light. Lobo Negro stayed behind with the pups. That was hard for Cocoa, but she knew it must be. The old wolf kept the pups playing right in front of the den, where they were not out in the open. The pack had traveled close to a mile from the den, and night was slowly falling. While the wolves were hunting, there would be nothing in their minds but the job at hand. Spirit was in the lead, with the other three close behind, his sharp eyes had seen something in the distance. Stopping to better focus, he could see that it was elk, but there was no scent. Sensing the breeze on his face, they were not quite downwind from the elk. So the pack started circling around, and keeping their distance, till they were completely downwind.

Now they started moving closer to the group of elk. Going as far as they could under cover, there was a large female closest to them. But far enough from cover, that they would be seen, before they could reach her. The elk were moving slowly away, so the pack sprang into action. The herd seeing the charging wolves, quickly took flight, Even Running at full speed, with the older She Wolf dropping behind, the other three barely caught her. All catching and holding on to the elks back legs, slowing her down enough, for She Wolf to catch up and grab a front leg. The animal now stumbled and fell, letting Spirit and Little Sister go for the kill. The three wolves holding on to the back of the elk, were shaken up and were tired and sore, but would be okay.

The pack had to lie down for a while to rest before they could eat their kill. After eating their fill, leaving a large piece for Lobo Negro, the pack started back to the den. She Wolf picked up the meat for Lobo

Negro, and the tired wolves traded off carrying it, several times before they got back. Upon reaching the den Cocoa and Spirit were glad to see their three pups were ok. Lobo Negro had kept them close in front of the den the whole time the pack was gone. While Lobo Negro ate the meat they brought back, the rest of the wolves were playing with the little ones. The two females, Grace and Gracie, were still looking much the same, both were grey and black. But Gracie had more black on her head. Hunter, the male, was a little more black then grey, and was larger than his sisters. Also, only one of his eyes was turning yellow. The other looked like it was going to stay blue, as all baby wolves are born with blue eyes. After Lobo Negro finished eating, there was still a little meat left on the bone for the pups to chew on. They are now becoming weaned from their mother, and will soon be going to a rendezvous site while the pack is hunting. When the young wolves were tired of chewing on the bone, they were ready to sleep as was the rest of the pack.

After another week had past, the pups were getting bigger and it was time to take them to a rendezvous site, while the pack hunted. When the pack went out to hunt this night there would be eight of them. The older wolves began to howl, and the young ones excitedly joined in as best they could. The pack started out with three wolves in front of, and two in back of the young wolves, so they couldn't stray. About a half mile or so from the den, they picked a rendezvous site. Tonight, still fearing for her pups, Cocoa wanted both Lobo Negro and She wolf, staying with her pups, and the other three would hunt. So Spirit, Little Sister, and Cocoa, left to hunt. It wasn't far from where they left the others, when the three caught the scent of deer. The wind was in their favor, blowing straight at them.

Moving slowly off in that direction, they soon saw several deer in a small clearing. Picking the largest buck, they moved very, very slowly through the cover to get closer. Crouching down, coiling all their muscles to the limit, the wolves exploded out of cover towards the buck. The deer hearing the crashing brush, bolted away, but not fast enough to out run the wolves. The trio quickly ran down the buck, two on the legs and the other on the neck, the strong jaws crushing its spine. After the kill, the wolves howled to let the others know to come. When the rest of the pack arrived, the three would try and track down the deer again, as this was not enough to feed them all. Fortunately the deer had not run too far before they stopped, about a half a mile. Making certain of the wind and cover, the wolves inched closer to the deer. There was another large buck that they would go for, again launching themselves out of cover. However, this time the deer were on the alert.

The buck they were after and another one behind him, spun around, antlers down in defense, while the rest of the deer ran off. The wolves quickly split apart around the two remaining, but Little Sister could not completely miss the antlers, bruising, but not cutting, her left hip. The pack was not yet giving up, and the three of them spread apart around the two bucks, waiting for an opening. One of the two deer panicked and decided it was time to run. The wolves didn't chase that one, because they would have the other behind them. This startled the remaining buck, giving the pack a split second opening, and they all charged in. One grabbed a front leg, one a back leg, and one the throat for the kill. The deer was quickly subdued, and the three sat down and howled, letting the other wolves know they were successful.

The trio then started eating their kill. Soon Lobo Negro and She Wolf appeared with the pups. She Wolf was carrying a leg bone that still had some meat on it for the young wolves that were trying to hold on to it as she walked. Cocoa stopped eating, to check on her pups when they arrived, seeing they were well, she returned to eating. When they all had eaten their fill, and the little ones finished tearing meat off the bones, the pack started back to the den. They again kept some members in front of, and some behind the pups, to make sure they were watched at all times. It had been a long night, but a safe and successful one. Upon reaching the den, the contented wolves were quickly asleep.

Chapter 11
For Little Sister

A few more weeks had passed. The pups were now twelve weeks old, and ready to go on hunts with the pack. As they started out on a hunt this night, the males as always, stopped briefly along the way to mark their territory. This was an example for the young wolves, and Spirit made sure that Hunter did the same. The pack had gone a fair way, and had not stopped at a rendezvous site. The pups, especially Hunter, were getting excited, thinking they were going on the hunt. The adults stopped, they had noticed the scent of elk, and were reading the signs. When they started out again, it was now time to keep the young wolves calm, and have them follow their lead. Getting close to where the elk would be, the adults slowed down, and the pups quietly followed their example.

The surrounding brush was tall enough that they didn't need to crouch down, and the pack slowly inched forward. When the elk came in view, the excited Hunter let out a bark, and the elk, of course, took flight. Spirit, quickly and quietly gave him a sharp nip, to calm him down. The elk really didn't know what had spooked them, and didn't run far. Again the pack slowly stalked the elk. There was a large female very close to the cover of brush. This time the young wolves were quiet, and in control, as the adults shot out surrounding the female. Lobo Negro and She Wolf grabbed her back legs and the other three a front leg, and the neck and throat. She struggled briefly, and was overcome and fell. The wolves quickly looked for attacking males, but the other elk had all run off.

The pups were still under cover and somewhat scared, by the size of the elk, and the fury of the kill. They were called out, and all joined in howling before they ate.

When the pack stopped howling, they heard a distant howl trailing off after theirs. The wolves, at this time, were not too concerned, but it needed to be kept in mind. After consuming a good meal, the pack started back toward the den. They would first go the pond to drink on the way, and were bounding along at a good pace.

Cocoa was at the back, still keeping a watchful eye on her pups. When they reached the pond, they no longer needed to wonder about the howl they heard earlier.

There, was a young male wolf, about three years old. He was a light black and grey, with areas of a light reddish brown color, and his name was Rusty. He had left his pack about a week ago, because he didn't agree with the Alpha male, and wanted to mate. So he was wandering, looking for a new life. Little Sister was the first to venture over to him, and touch noses and smell him, as he did her. Little Sister had also been thinking about a mate, lately, and time would tell.

The rest of the pack was now getting to know Rusty, and he them. There didn't seem to be any problem with any of the wolves accepting him, and after drinking they returned to the den. Cocoa and Spirit and the pups, went into their den, and the rest of the pack in theirs. For now, Rusty lay down outside, between the dens, and all were soon asleep.

The next evening when the wolves awoke and came out of their dens, they greeted

Rusty, as now one of the pack. And all took turns, sniffing noses, and getting more familiar with their new member. When Little Sister greeted Rusty, she licked him affectionately on his muzzle, letting him know she was interested in him as a mate. This made Rusty very happy, because that's why he was on this journey. He bounced around several times, giving a few excited barks, and came back to rub his head and shoulders on Little sister.

He also was a welcome addition to the pack, as another young hunter, because Lobo Negro and She Wolf were quickly ageing. So they now had four young, strong hunters, Rusty, Little Sister, Cocoa and Spirit. Also Cocoa's pups were starting to go on the hunts, and would soon be learning to hunt. Now that all the excitement calmed down the wolves started a vigorous howling session, to start the hunt. The pack bounded off into the falling darkness, with a renewed energy, with Little Sister and Rusty in the lead. After running for a ways, they slowed down as it got darker, and soon caught the scent of elk. The pack stopped briefly, to sense the breeze, and figure out where the elk should be. They moved off in that direction, slowly now, as the scent got stronger. The pack continued moving slower and slower, until they were now just inching forward. They could hear the sound of the elk, moving around in the brush, just ahead. Now the animals were taking shape, seen through the cover of brush, hiding the wolves from the elk.

At the same time that they saw the elk, the pack exploded into action, encircling a large female that was facing away from the attacking wolves. The four younger wolves were at the front, while the two older ones had caught the rear legs. With six wolves on her, the elk quickly fell. As she hit the ground the pack quickly looked up, to see two charging males, coming at them. They instantly turned and ran, some leaping over the carcass. Putting it between the charging males and themselves gave them just enough gain to get safely away, without injury. The pack ran, until they could no longer hear the elk, crashing through the brush, behind them. Slowing down, while looking over their shoulders, to make sure the elk were not there, they stopped, carefully listening as they caught their breath. The pups that were still under the cover of brush, when all this happened, fortunately started running as soon as they saw the rest of the pack running, which kept them out of harms- way.

The wolves now started back to where they had left their kill. As they approached the area, they saw no sign of the rest of the elk, which had moved on. They could now relax and eat their meal. Rusty let out a howl for the successful hunt and the rest of the pack joined in. After leisurely eating their fill, the contented wolves sat licking their mouths. Little Sister also licked Rusty on his muzzle, and rubbed her head against him, in a show of affection. It was obvious that they were now a pair. On the way back to the den, Hunter now stopped here and there, to mark his territory, without being shown by his father. As usual the pack stopped at the pond to drink, before continuing to the den. When they reached the den, Rusty, now knowing his place with Little Sister and the pack, went into the den with the rest.

Cocoa's pups were now reaching seven months old, their milk teeth had been replaced with adult teeth, and they were now ready to join in on the hunt. The young

wolves would not be pushed into the kill,
but would join in instinctively when ready.
As the wolves awoke this night and came
out of their den, they yawned, stretched, and
howled to start another hunt. Tonight the
pack headed down towards the valley floor,
where they hadn't been for a while. About
half way down, the scent of elk was on the
breeze. The wind was coming from their
left, so they turned off in that direction. In a
few more minutes, the scent got stronger,
and the pack slowed down, and looked and
listened. They could hear the elk, but not
yet see them, so they inched closer till they
could.

As the elk became visible through the
brush, there were seven or eight in the
group. They picked out a female that was
closest, and sprang into action. The four
younger wolves reached her first, and Lobo
Negro and She wolf were close behind,

adding more weight to bring her down. At this point Hunter, the male pup, charged out to help. Also at the same time a male elk came running at them with deadly antlers down. He was close, heading straight at Hunter, She Wolf, without thinking, threw herself between the elk and Hunter. The large male elk caught her at full speed, throwing her into the air, and almost trampling Hunter. The rest of the pack stood their ground teeth bared growling ferociously at the elk. The elk standing there facing this display, must have decided he had done his job, turned and left.

Lobo Negro went to She Wolf, his long-time mate, licking her face as she took her last breath. He lay down with his head on hers, deeply mourning this tragic loss. The rest of the pack gathered around, also mourning this loss. But life must go on, and the pack fed on their kill, all except Lobo Negro. When the rest of the pack was done eating, Lobo Negro was still laying with his head on She Wolf. When they turned to go, he did not follow. They turned and whined for him to come, but he did not. The wolves returned and started digging a hole next to She Wolf. When it was large enough, they, not knowing what would happen, dragged her into it. Lobo Negro watched as they did this, without objecting, and they covered her up.

This seemed to break the bond with the body, but not the soul, and the memory. Lobo Negro now ate  some of the elk, and the pack slowly and sadly returned to the den.

Chapter 12
The Last Journey

Lobo Negro awoke the next morning, without much sleep, the memory of She Wolf weighed heavy on his mind. He had been planning for himself and She Wolf, to spend their last days with the Indian, when Cocoa's pups were a little older. Well, now they were, and they missed it by a day. Also Rusty was now there, to help with the hunting, so the pack was in good balance. And so without looking back, he started off to the Indian. Slowly at first, then breaking into a trot, he could feel her there beside him. He never got as close to the Indian as Spirit did on their last visit, but had felt the bond from the first time he saw him.

Looking forward to this, and needing something new to fill his mind, Lobo Negro picked up the pace to an easy stretched out lope, but after a while, he could feel the tiredness of age slowing him down, and dropped back to a trot. Stopping at a small pond, he took his time drinking and catching his breath, before trotting off again on the path to Stands Alone.

It was now afternoon when he reached the clearing where his friend lived. As he stepped out of the brush, he saw the Indian smoking meat from a deer he had killed that morning.

"My oldest friend, the black wolf, you have returned, and alone. I must assume you have lost your mate. I am sorry for your loss, but also glad it has brought you back to me. The Great Spirit works in strange ways."

Lobo Negro felt warmth and comfort in the Indian's voice, and walked over and sat down next to him.

"I have a nice piece of fresh meat, I have not yet put on the fire," he said while stroking the big wolf's head, "it must be for you."

Lobo Negro was hungry from the journey, and not eating much yesterday.

As the wolf ate the meat, the Indian watched him, his heart filled with joy and pride, at this gift that the Great Spirit had brought him.

Back at the den, Spirit woke up in the early afternoon. Walking out of the den, he noticed Lobo Negro was not around. He knew where he probably had gone, but first went to the pond to make sure. It was no surprise that he wasn't there. As he drank, he knew that the old wolf had gone to the

Indian, for his final days. On his way back to the den, he thought he would take the pack, if they wanted to follow, to his friend that had named him. He remembered that his father had taken him there, when he was a young wolf, and wanted to do the same.

When back at the den, he gave a sharp bark to wake up the others. As the pack came out and stretched and yawned, they also noticed Lobo Negro was not there. Little Sister knew as did Spirit, that their father had gone to the Indian. She went to the pond to drink as did the rest of the pack, knowing that Spirit would go and she would follow. Cocoa and her pups would of course follow Spirit, not knowing where they were going, and Rusty would follow Little Sister. So the pack of now seven, started out with only two, knowing where they were going. Spirit led the way with an easy, bounding lope, for young wolves it's a joy to run like that.

The pack kept up the pace for the first hour, then settled down to a trot for a while, pausing for the males to mark the trail, now and then. Later on when they stopped at the pond, where Lobo Negro had stopped to drink, they also quenched their thirst. When the wolves left the pond, they ran at an easy lope for the rest of the way. Reaching the Indian's tepee early evening while it was still light, Spirit immediately walked over to Lobo Negro and the Indian, touching noses with the old wolf.

"Now I am truly blessed with the whole family, and my friend Spirit has returned." said the Indian, while rubbing Spirit's head. Little Sister had followed Spirit over, to rub noses with Lobo Negro, also.

"You are braver this time Little Sister, with a wisdom that comes from maturity."

The rest of the pack was still at the edge of the clearing, not knowing what to make of this unfamiliar situation. Lobo Negro got up and walked over to the other wolves, sniffing noses and rubbing around them. This was like a goodbye that he hadn't done at the den. Spirit and little Sister came back from greeting the Indian, and again rubbed noses and heads with Lobo Negro. They knew they would not see him again and this was goodbye. The pack disappeared into the brush and would hunt as they got back closer to the den.

Lobo Negro returned to the Indian and lay down near him.

"We have all said our goodbyes my brother, and we will have each-other's company for a while. I will enjoy and remember the time we have, for the rest of my life, as long as the Great Spirit wills it."

Lobo Negro was tired from the journey today. And was quickly asleep, probably dreaming of the first time he and She Wolf were here, when they first came to this valley.

Stands Alone was also soon asleep, dreaming of his gift, of sharing his life, with his brother the wolf.

The wolf pack was about halfway back to the den, when they came across the scent of elk. Stopping to read the signs, the elk should be still ahead of them on the way home. After a while, as the scent got stronger, they slowed down knowing they were close. Spirit was the first to see the elk, stopping on point, signaling the rest of the pack. The four adults spread out on each side of him, with the three young wolves behind. Launching themselves out of cover to the nearest female, Rusty and Little Sister grabbed the hind legs, Spirit the throat, with Cocoa on the neck. The three young wolves had followed them out, and were all trying to grab something. The elk had tried to run, but didn't get far, and was dragged down by the weight of the wolves.

The pack quickly looked up for attacking males, but luckily, they had all run off. Hunter, Grace, and Gracie, filled with excitement from participating in their first hunt, started howling, with the rest of the pack joining in. After consuming a good meal, the pack trotted off again on the journey home. The pack as usual stopped at the pond to drink, then continued back to the den. It had been a long day and night, and an interesting one for some, with the contact to the Indian. And life would be a little different now, without Lobo Negro and

She Wolf, but it is all taken in stride, as a part of life. Reaching the den, a very tired wolf pack went to sleep.

Chapter 13
Life Goes On

Lobo Negro awoke the next morning, and raised his head to look at his new surroundings. Remembering where he was, and getting here yesterday, he stood up, stretched, and yawned. As he did this, Stands Alone stepped out of his tepee, saying,

"Good morning my brother, I trust you slept well. We are at the beginning of a new day, in a new life."

As he did this he walked over to the wolf, rubbing his head.

"We will have to figure this out as we go along, for it is new to both of us. Come, I will show you where the nearest water is."

The Indian said this, as he walked away. He looked back and saw Lobo Negro was not following.

"Come, my friend."

He said, as he motioned with his arm, and his head. Now the big wolf understood and walked along next to his friend. They walked quietly along, for a short way, coming to a small stream that ran along through the valley floor.

"I am sure you could have found it by yourself, but it gives me time to think as we walked."

The Indian kneeled down, scooping up water to drink, out of his hand. And Lobo Negro stood, drinking beside him.

After drinking Lobo Negro raised his head, the breeze coming from across the stream, was bringing the scent of deer to him. He crossed the stream and disappeared into the brush on the other side.

"Good hunting, my brother." The Indian whispered, wondering, and hoping, the wolf would still be fast enough. He turned and started back to his tepee to have his breakfast.

Lobo Negro had gone about a quarter of a mile, when he sensed the deer were close. Crouching down he inched forward, until he saw the deer through the brush. There were three or four of them, and a doe was closest to him. Fortunately, there was not a lot of distance, between the deer and him. Digging in his feet, and coiling his muscles, he exploded out of cover to the deer. They took flight at the noise of brush breaking, but were close enough that he could catch her and bring her down. His still powerful jaws quickly killing his prey, and he threw back his head and gave a long howl.

The Indian, hearing this, jumped up breakfast in hand, saying

"He has done it, he is telling the world of his hunt."

Stands Alone sat back down, finishing his breakfast.

And a very happy wolf was having his meal for the day.

Lobo Negro finished eating, and sat licking his mouth, thinking of She Wolf, and wishing she was still with him. And in a way she was. He got up, urinated around the deer, and trotting back across the stream to his friend's tepee, marking the way as he went.

When he arrived the Indian greeted him, saying,

"I am proud of you my brother. You are still a great hunter."

The words sounded good to Lobo Negro, and a contended wolf lay down near his friend and took a nap.

That evening back at the wolf pack, they came out, stretched and yawned getting ready for another nights hunt. Rusty was very happy he had found Little sister for a mate, and rubbed against her to show it, and she returned it. He was also glad he found a pack that didn't have an alpha male, that wouldn't allow other males to mate. It was more a group of pairs that worked together, for the common good. Little Sister feeling very happy bounded off in the lead, with Rusty and the rest close behind. It's a beautiful thing when wolves run happy together, just to be running. The pack slowed down as the night got darker, all their keen senses searching for the scent of game.

Suddenly it was there, the scent of elk. Stopping to feel the soft breeze coming from up wind, they knew which direction the elk would be. Starting off again, trotting at first, and then slowing down as the scent got stronger. Spirit now in the lead, slowly creeping ever closer, stopped when he could see them through the brush. There were eight elk, four of them males, so the wolves must be ready for an attack, from them. They watched for a while, until a large female started wandering away from the males. The pack slowly and quietly moved away with her. When the time was right, seven wolves surrounded her bringing her down for the kill. Spirit, who had a leg in his teeth, looked up to see the males charging towards them.

He let out a loud bark, alerting the rest to run, and they did, fast and furious. In a little ways it got quiet behind them, and the pack stopped to look back. The male elk had quit and were walking slowly back to the rest. The wolves followed at a safe distance, watching for the elk to move off. When they were out of sight, the pack went back to their kill. The three young wolves started to howl, but the adults quickly stopped them, not wanting to bring back the male elk. The pack took their time having a good meal, and then trotted off back to the pond, and the den. It was now starting to get light, as morning was coming, and the pack would sleep till the next night.

Lobo Negro woke up from his nap, and saw Stands Alone sitting in front of his tepee, eating some smoked deer meat for his lunch. Maybe the smell of that is what woke him up.

"Did you have a good nap my brother?"

The Indian said, throwing him a piece of meat, which he caught in his mouth.

"When we finish this, I must work on my new moccasins that I am making."

He threw the wolf another piece of meat that he caught.

Lobo Negro got up and decided he would go out exploring around this area, which he had not done yet. He went out into the brush around the clearing, going about a mile away from it. Then he started a big circle around the area, marking his trail as he went. He found himself missing She Wolf beside him. They had come to this valley together, and had never been apart. He also found he was missing the other wolves, and wondered if he should be here. It was getting later in the day now, and shadows were starting. This is the time of day, when other animals are starting to come out exploring also.

He came to the stream that runs through the valley, and had seen something moving in the shadows, about a quarter mile away. Turning quickly back into the brush, and circling around to where he thought it was. The wind felt like it was coming from that direction, so he didn't think he had been detected. When he crept through the brush near the stream, he soon saw a few deer drinking from it. He wasn't on a hunt, but they were very close, so he decided not to waste it. Calling on all the energy in an old body, he sprang from cover after the deer. They took flight when they saw him, running as hard as he could. He couldn't catch them.

He stopped, panting now from the energy he had spent, it felt like it had drained him. Sitting down to catch his breath, he wondered what was coming now.

Chapter 14
A period of Adjustment

When Lobo Negro had caught his breath, he stood up realizing he probably had, had, his last hunt. Feeling very tired, and exploring done for the day, he followed the stream back to the Indian's tepee. Walking into the light of the fire, his tail and head hanging down, his friend could see something had happened.

He said, "Something has caused you this pain, my brother. I think maybe you tried to hunt, and failed. If this is so, do not worry my friend, I will hunt for us both."

As he said this, he walked to the old wolf, rubbing the sides of his head with both hands as one would a loved dog, and realizing just how big this animal was.

"I will have my meal now, and I know you ate the deer this morning, so you don't need much. But we will eat and you will see you don't have to worry."

The Indian went to get smoked meat, where he had it hanging in a tree, to keep animals from getting it. He also got roots, from plants that he knew were nourishing, from his tepee.

Lobo Negro lie watching and listening, as his friend was doing this, and it seemed to give him comfort.

Stands Alone cut a good sized piece off the meat, for the wolf, which he gave to him, saying,

"Eat this, my brother. You will see you don't have to worry. We will hunt again tomorrow, and get more fresh meat."

The unlikely pair quietly ate the meal, each watching the other, and learning. This was the same meat the Indian gave him pieces of before. It was different then fresh, and tasted strange, but it was good.

When they finished eating, Stands Alone could see the wolf was very tired, and he went into his tepee.

He called, "Come my brother, sleep in here with me tonight, it will be warm, like your den."

He called to the wolf several times, patting the ground as he did. Lobo Negro understood and got up and walked in and lay down. The Indian sat next to him for a while, rubbing his head, and marveling at this gift the Great Spirit had given him. Stands Alone got up, and went outside to smoke his pipe for a while before going to bed, but stayed where the wolf could see him. Soon he came in and went to sleep, marveling at this great gift.

The wolf pack was out on a hunt tonight with Hunter, the young male in the lead. The adults were letting him try for his first time. Looking much like a full grown wolf, as the pups do after six months, he looked sure of himself, and felt so. His two sisters, Grace and Gracie being not yet as confidant, were mingled with the pack. Spirit was close behind Hunter, just in case, but he too felt confident about his son. The young wolf now stopped, finding the scent of elk on the breeze. He studied the way the wind felt on his face, knowing the direction he started off again at a trot. As the scent got stronger, he slowed down, moving carefully ahead, senses straining for answers.

Now he saw something through the surrounding brush, and stopped. Creeping forward he could see elk taking shape.

There were several, and fortunately a large female was closest, and the two males, were farther away on the other side. He didn't hesitate, and sprang into action. He charged out grabbing a hind leg, Spirit right behind him, catching the other, the rest of the pack attacking legs, neck, and throat, as she struggled to move, with seven wolves, bringing her down. The wolves looked up from their kill, expecting charging males, but there were none. The rest of the elk had run off. Hunter, seeing this began to howl for his first conquest as a hunter, living up to his name.

After a long howling session that could be heard for miles, the pack enjoyed a good meal. Hunter sat down licking his mouth with satisfaction, feeling twice his size. Maybe as big as Lobo Negro, who he wouldn't forget. When the wolves were done eating, they rubbed around each other, knitting the group ever tighter. The pack bounded off through the night, feeling good, feeling free, and content. When they stopped at the pond to drink, the younger ones were splashing around in the water, and all joined in the play. Playing is a side of wolves not always seen, but a necessary part of life. When at the den the pack lay down close together, falling into a bonding sleep.

Lobo Negro woke up the next morning, in the tepee. As he lifted his head and opened his eyes, it took a second or two to remember, that's where he was. He saw Stands Alone still asleep, and thought it was not unlike being with another wolf. She Wolf crept into his mind again, and he wished she was here to share this, but she was always as close as his thoughts. He stood up, and he had regained some of his strength back, and no longer felt so weak. This made him feel better, but he knew he was done hunting. Stepping out of the tepee was like coming out of a den, so the old wolf knew he would be comfortable there at night. He walked towards the stream, and saw three deer there drinking. Knowing he could no longer catch them, he wished the Indian was awake and there. At that instant something swished past his ear, and one of the deer fell.

He turned his head to see him standing there, holding that curved stick he had seen on his shoulder in the past. The other two deer had run off, and Stands Alone and the wolf walked together to the dead deer. The Indian bent down, and pulled a stick out of the deer. Seeing this Lobo Negro thought, somehow the long curved stick, made the short stick fly to the deer. That's what he heard go by his ear, and it pierced the deer like his teeth and killed it. His friend was holding the short stick in his hand, and the end looked like a tooth.

The Indian looked at the big wolf and said,

"I told you, you need not worry, I would hunt for us both."

The wise old wolf looked at him as if he understood, and probably did.

Lobo Negro had not noticed, but the Indian woke up as he went out of the tepee, and came out behind him. Then he too saw the deer, and he quickly grabbed his bow and arrow, and let fly.

"Come my brother, you carry my bow and arrow," as he placed it in his mouth,

"And I will carry the deer."

Stands Alone picked up the deer, hefting it on his shoulder. They walked like the good friends that they were, to the tree where a rope was waiting to hang the deer.

Taking the bow and arrow from the wolf's mouth, he said. "Thank you for carrying that for me, it saved me a trip."

He placed the bow at the tepee and came back to the deer. Tying the rope around the deer's antlers, he pulled it off the ground. After tying off the rope, he took out his knife, and deftly cut the deer open from chest to tail. The entrails came falling out, and he cut them loose from the deer.

"Could you clean those up for me my brother?" he said, pointing to them, on the ground.

And the wolf willingly did.

He then quickly and expertly, skinned the deer. Hanging the hide on the tree, he would tan it later. Then he cut a front leg and shoulder from the deer, placing it on the ground in front of the wolf.

He said, "There my brother. That should finish your meal for the day."

While Lobo Negro ate the meat off the bone, and was engrossed in chewing on the bone. The Indian cut another leg and shoulder from the deer, along with the rear leg bones, wrapped them in hide, and hung it from the tree for tomorrow. He then cut the other portions of meat from the carcass, and put them on a skewer, made from a smooth stick, to smoke over the fire.

"Now, my brother, it is time for my meal." He said.

Chapter 15
An Ending and a Beginning

Stands Alone fixed his morning meal,
some smoked or jerky meat, and some
roots and berries, and whatever other
nourishing things he could find. It was a
simple life, working in harmony with nature.
Now of course, his life was much, more,
full, with Lobo Negro with him, for
whatever the length of time...this he would
cherish. The big wolf had been chewing on
the leg bone, while his friend was eating.
And now he seemed to be content with that,
and his eyes closed for a little nap.

Stands Alone took the deer skin off the
tree, and stretched it out on a grassy area,
with sticks pounded into the ground. He

then spread dry sand on it to dry it out. Salt worked best, but he had none. He would leave it there for a few days, and then work on tanning it. Then he would make clothes or bags or whatever he needed at the time.

After a while Lobo Negro woke up from his nap, got up and stretched and yawned, and walked to the stream to drink. When he returned the Indian said,

"Why don't we go for a walk my brother, it is always good to know what is going on around us."

The wolf didn't know what he said, but followed him.

They walked quietly along for quite a while, words were not necessary. Lobo Negro would stop now and then, to mark his territory. Stands Alone knew the wolf was old and tired, so he carefully watched for signs that they needed to go back. After about two miles, the Indian knew it was time.

He said "Let us rest here for a little while." as he sat down on a big rock.

Lobo Negro lay down watching his friend, and listening.

"It is good to just sit and watch the world move around you. We are but a small part of it, and it lets us share it for a brief lifetime. None of us know how long we will be here. Your lifetime is much shorter than mine, but it is your plan, chosen by nature."

The Indian talked like this for a while, and thought it was good to talk to someone, other than your-self.

The wolf lie watching him, and listening. He didn't know the words, but the sound was very pleasant.

Soon Stands Alone stood up and said.

"Let us start back my friend. I have enjoyed this walk with you, more than you could know."

The pair walked silently back to the tepee, each lost in the river of their own thoughts.

The wolf pack had awakened in late afternoon. They were outside the den, visiting, and relaxing, before the nights hunt. The young wolves, were running around chasing each other, and sometimes would get the adults involved, or get a sharp nip, when they weren't in the mood. This night the two sisters, Grace and Gracie, started to howl for time to start the hunt. When the howling was done, the pair bounded off in the lead, indicating they wanted to lead the hunt. Even though the pack works as a hunting machine, the individual wants to find their own strength. The sisters were after that tonight. Rusty and Little Sister had jumped in behind their daughters, as back up for their first lead. The pack had gone about a mile, when Grace stopped nose in the air. The scent of elk was fairly strong, so she carefully studied the signs of wind and smell coming to her. Gracie also doing this looked at her sister in agreement, as they set out, slowly now, in the direction they knew the elk were.

Soon the scent was flooding their noses, so they stopped, studied, and then crept forward, until they saw the animals through the cover. The closest elk was a large male. To the left was a good sized female, a little farther away from the male, and still upwind. The pair slowly worked their way closer to their intended prey. When in position, the two leapt out, charging at the elk grabbing the hind legs. Rusty and Little

Sister behind them went for the neck and throat, the others grabbing legs and nose to bring her down. As they did this the male had wheeled around to attack. The wolves looked up to see him charging at them. They quickly split up running in different directions confusing the elk, which slowed down enough to let them escape.

The elk stopped, as he saw the pack of wolves splitting into seven different quickly fading targets. The pack rejoined and slowly walked back, until they saw the elk had gone. Grace and Gracie started the howling, happy with the fact that they proved themselves as hunters. It wouldn't matter if they ever did it again or not. The other wolves rubbed in and out among the two in approval, then feasted on the kill. When done, the pack trotted off to the pond, and then to the den to rest. After reaching the den, Grace and Gracie were still so excited from their success with the hunt. They began to howl all over again, the pair kept it up for almost two minutes. The other wolves could not help but join in, and all understood. The pair slept as one that night.

Lobo Negro and Stands Alone arrived back at the tepee early evening. The Indian could see the old wolf was tired, and said,

"Let me start a fire and we will have our meal, then we can rest afterwards."

When the fire was going, he went and got the meat down from the tree. He took the shoulder and leg, along with the back leg bones, out of the skins and gave them to the wolf. While Lobo Negro was eating, he cut himself a portion of meat, and wrapped and hung the remaining meat, then gathered some roots and berries, and sat down to eat.

"This will make a nice end to a perfect day my brother."

The two ate their meal in silence. When Lobo Negro was done, he got up, went to the Indian and licked his hand, then went into the tepee and fell asleep. A broad smile crossed the Indians face, and no words were necessary, nor could they describe the feeling. Stands Alone lit his pipe with a brand from the fire. He smoked it for quite a long time, while lost in thoughts, of wonder and joy. Then went into the tepee and lay down, with the thoughts still going, giving way to peaceful sleep.

The wolf and the Indian had now fallen into a routine of sorts, with eating, talking, and walking and hunting when necessary. This went on for a few weeks, and was a pleasant time for both.

Little Sister, now carrying Rusty's pups, knew it would not be long before they were delivered. The pack was outside of the dens, this afternoon. With Lobo Negro and She

Wolf gone, the large den would be big enough for Spirit, Cocoa, and, the three young wolves. The smaller would be fine for her, and the pups, and Rusty. When the pack hunted tonight, she would go along, but not participate in the kill. Tonight Hunter started the howling for the hunt, and would again lead the pack for the second time, now that his sisters had been successful. It was part of the training, for the young wolves to lead the hunt, so they could become more proficient hunters.

The rest of the pack, all joined in with the howling, before the hunt. When they were done, Hunter loped off into the falling darkness with the rest behind. About a mile from the den, he noticed the faint scent of elk, the breeze on his face gave him the direction. The fact that the scent was faint, told him the elk were still far away, so he ran off in that direction. As the scent grew stronger, he started slowing down. Now, he could tell they were close, he crept ahead. As the elk took shape through the cover, he saw six or seven feeding. There was a male right in front of him, and two large females to the far right.

Working his way towards the females behind cover was very slow, but necessary. Finally the pack was in position, Hunter shot out at the far female with the pack around him, except Little Sister, who stayed behind. He let the others grab legs, while he went for the neck for the kill. Spirit went for the throat to make sure. Little Sister, who was watching, saw a male elk charging towards the pack. She started barking, giving an early warning. The pack split in seven different directions as they ran away, and it worked again, like the last time. The elk gave up with too many targets to follow. When it was safe, the pack returned, and had their meal, and later returned to the den, with Hunter again feeling very proud of the hunt.

As the weeks passed, Stands Alone could see the wolf tiring more and more, and knew the end was not far off. This morning he woke up before Lobo Negro, and was outside getting the meat down from the tree, when the old wolf came out. Lobo Negro sat down where he usually ate, and the Indian put down a portion in front of him. As he did this the wolf licked his hand, this always brought a lump up in his throat, especially today.

"We have become very close, like two brothers." The Indian said.

"I am going to miss you terribly." He added.

The two ate quietly together, the wolf laying on the ground, and the Indian sitting next to him. When they finished, Stands Alone was rubbing him on his head and neck, still amazed at the size of this one hundred and seventy pound animal. He did this for the next fifteen or twenty minutes, their eyes locked together, with the love of true friends. Stands Alone got up, putting things away from their meal. The wolf lay with his head on his paws watching him.

At the den, Little Sister was in the back of the den giving birth to four little pups. After licking the sack from their heads as they were born, she ate the placenta and was cleaning them one by one. Then she was encouraging them to nurse, one by one, and the last one wasn't moving. She moved it around with her nose and her paw, but it was lifeless. This is not unusual with births, as the mortality rate is high. When she was sure it was dead, she whined and barked, calling Rusty to her side. He watched her nuzzling the lifeless pup, and did so himself, and knew it was dead. He gently picked it up, and carried it outside, away from the den. After digging a hole under a tree, he nuzzled it again to make sure, and picked it up, dropping it in the hole, covering it up.

Lobo Negro had walked to the stream to drink. When he was done, he started back to the tepee, but feeling suddenly very tired, he sat down and started a howl that was terribly mournful.

At the same time, Rusty started the same kind of a mournful howl, the two cries meeting in the middle of the valley, filling it with sorrow.

When Lobo Negro stopped, he lay down, as the life left him, and as he closed his eyes, he saw She Wolf waiting for him with two small pups. One was Spirits, killed by the eagle, the other Little Sisters, whose spirit was much bigger than the vessel it just left. Hearing this mournful howling, Stands Alone knew what had happened. He came to his brother, knelt down beside him, tears running down his face, falling on Lobo Negro, and said, "Goodbye my brother, my friend, you and the Great Spirit, have given me a gift, far greater than any other."

He left and got a crude shovel he had made from a branch, and dug a shallow hole next to the wolf. Dragging the big wolf in, the tears still running, he covered him, and then collected rocks covering the grave.

"There my brother, I will visit you every day for the rest of my life."

And so it is in nature, lives are lost and more are started.